The Apology You Never Got

© **Bridgette Alese Ferguson** January 2021
Beautiful Hearts & Bold Attitudes, Inc.

All right reserved. No portion of this book may be reproduced, stored in a retrieval system, or transmitted in any form or by any means—electronic, mechanical, photocopy, recording, scanning, or other—except for brief quotations in critical reviews or articles, without the prior written permission of the publisher.

Unless otherwise noted, most Scripture quotations marked KJV are from the King James Version of the Bible or NIV are from the New International Version of the Bible.

Book Designed by kreativeroots.com

Cover Photography by T. Marquis Management & Services, LLC.

Proofreading by Lydia Hyslop

Edited by Enam Jarrar Jordan

The Apology You Never Got

Reflect! Be inspired! Enter this season with forgiveness!

BRIDGETTE ALESE FERGUSON

Dedication

This book is dedicated to my Lord and Savior Jesus Christ. Thank you for always allowing me to find a friend in you. Thank you for being a true example of how love, forgiveness, and reconciliation should be in my faith and values. Thank you for your patience with me to write this book as you have instructed. It has not been easy but more rewarding knowing that this is what you want as I surrender to your will and your ways for my life. Thank you for your continued unfailing love, mercy, grace, patience, and faithfulness that continues to carry me through. To God be all the glory, honor, and praise!

To my husband, Tyler Marquis Ferguson, I thank God for you as you truly are an answered prayer. The Lord has used you to preserve and challenge me in my faith. Our family couldn't be more proud to have you leading us by the wisdom of God that rests upon you for our legacy.

To my dear children, thank you for loving your mommy with unconditional love. Constantly telling me just how special and valuable I am to you is a daily reflection of God's love and a reminder of why I am here. As I pray for the wisdom and discernment of God over your life, may you always be humble, do what's right, and stay close to Him, knowing that you will never go wrong or be led astray as long as he comes first. As you grow older and have families of your own, please stick by each other's side, forgiving one another always. Not only would this make your father and I happy but it would bring your father in heaven so much glory. Prayerfully, we will be the examples you have watched and learned from if moments to forgive should come to pass. I love you unconditionally and will always be there for you no matter the age or the hour.

Acknowledgments

To my parents, Tami and Alonzo Bell, you've always been there for me before I had family, and now after, with unconditional love and support. As a bonus dad, you have been a great blessing to our family. Being so used to disappointment, I gave you such a hard time because I thought you were going to fail our family. I'm sitting here in tears thinking about how some people have let me down but can't think of one time you were never able to come through for me when I needed you. Thank you so much for being the dad I never had. You both are wonderful to my children, and I am grateful for the bond you have with them. It means more than you know.

To my uncle and aunt, Carlton Ray Baker and Joyce Ann Richardson Baker (deceased), thank you for your help raising me to be the woman I am today with unconditional love and nurturing support. God used you both as key instruments to bring me to Christ Jesus as you showed me his unconditional love and continued acts of kindness. Thank you for showing me that marriages do exist and can get through anything with the Lord as your strength and strong tower.

To my sister, Jessica Leigh Jones, thank you for being the best aunt a nephew and niece could ever ask for. I can tell by the way they speak of you that your nurturing love and care is so sincere. For me to see it is one thing but for them to excitedly speak about it is another. Thank you for being there for our family during one of our life's moments of uncertainty. We are forever grateful for your support, sacrifice, and loyalty.

To my cousin and best friend, Pastor Enam Jarrar Jordan, thank you so much for inspiring and pushing me at my weakest. I don't have to be anyone but myself with you. Our genuine and down-to-earth relationship keeps me sane and refreshed. If no one understands me, I can always count on you to understand and hear me well, just like with Aunt Joyce when she was here on earth. Thank you for your loyalty, always making it easy for me to confide in you and bombarding the throne of God on my behalf of my family and me.

To aunt Emma Nesbitt **and my dear grandmothers,** Jannie Louise Scott and Janet Barber Nelson, who I love and honor, thank you so much for your unconditional love, grace, and favor you've always shown me. Your countless encouraging mailed cards and acts of thoughtfulness toward my family and I have ministered to me greatly, and I will forever be grateful. With all that each of you have been through when it comes to forgiving, you all make being the backbone and matriarch of our family look so easy. Grandma Louise, you instantly forgave my mother with no condemnation for having me in her teenage years and encouraged her to stay in school as you promised to help take care of me. I am beyond grateful to God for your heart and all the many sacrifices I've watched you make so that we could keep hot food on the table. Aunt Emma and Grandma Janet, your life truly witnesses and teaches me constantly how to love and treat people—even to those who have been unkind to you. You both are truly an example of Christ.

I honor and thank God for my Pastors and Covering, Brian and Tamika Duley. Thank you for both being a breath of fresh air to our family. Thank you for your transparency, teaching of the word, encouragement, and continued prayers. It is an honor to serve at Nikao Church with such humble and like-minded willing vessels who are on fire for God.

I honor and thank God for Apostle Cynthia Dumas-Cook, Prophet Michael Crawford, Apostle Dr. G. Marie Carroll, Apostle Maureen Manoly, Apostle Adrienne Castle, and Prophetess Phyllis Cunningham for allowing God to use each of you mightily to prophesy, counsel, mentor, love, and pray for me as the journey I've been called to has not been easy. I love each of you dearly. Thank you so much for your love, encouragement, and compassion towards my family and me; it will never go unnoticed.

Contents

Introduction   *13*

1: **Forgiving A Parent**   *17*

2: **Forgiving Your Spouse**   *23*

3: **Forgiving A Sibling**   *31*

4: **Forgiving A Work Colleague**   *37*

5: **Forgiving An Opportunist Disguised As A Friend**   *45*

6: **Forgiving A Mother-In-Law**   *53*

7: **Forgiving Yourself**   *65*

8: **My Apology To You**   *71*

About the Author   *77*

"They triumphed over him by the blood of the Lamb and by the word of their testimony; they did not love their lives so much as to shrink from death."

—Revelation 12:11

Introduction

This book has been written out of obedience to my Father in heaven. I did not write this book with any malicious motives, nor did I write it to offend, cause pain, or tear anyone down—which is why I chose not to expose names. This book was written to testify how God brought me through a flood of hurt, pain, and rejection by my willingness to forgive. I believe with all my heart that he wants to do it for you, too.

May the Lord clear your mind with peace and open your tender heart as you read this book with intent to heal, be delivered, and set free from that which the enemy has tried to keep you bound, ultimately robbing you. May each testimony not only transform you but also compel you to test God's word as you surrender through obedience to his will for your life, in Jesus' name. *Amen.*

Overcoming obstacles seems like it can be a huge mountain to climb sometimes, but when we do it, it feels great. When you've overcome huge heartbreaking experiences, it brings a new sense of freedom.
I have overcome many hindrances in life, praise be to God, and I want you to overcome, too. I have overcome rejection, abandonment, the spirit of promiscuity, fear of the unknown, superficial mindset, depression, and unforgiveness.

Out of all, interestingly, I actually think overcoming unforgiveness and rejection was the very hardest for me. Being promiscuous was a choice I made on my own in hopes to fill a void. The root of that was from abandonment and rejection—the need and pursuit to find love and feel accepted by a man since I was unable to get it from my biological father. Once I allowed God to deliver me from that spirit, it was easy to move on, but continually being rejected and having to deal with betrayal was something others inflicted upon me and took me longer to get over, more so because I didn't want to accept how I was mistreated by those I loved so much, or perhaps I expected some type of apology that I would never get.

After I started taking my walk with Christ more seriously, forgiving became extremely important to me, mostly so that God would forgive me as well as having a strong desire to be free in my heart. Unforgiveness keeps you bound and shackled up in the mind and heart. It's almost tormenting because it can actually do just as much harm on your body physically and internally due to stress. I've had to forgive loved ones from family to friends. It didn't come easily with every situation, but doing it was a must in order to retain a pure heart, protect my peace, and to be free in all things of God so that he can truly use me for his glory.

1. Forgiving A Parent

The role of a present parent is so important to a child's life. A good father brings structure, inner peace, high esteem, and confidence that allows the child to be more effective in the year-to-year goals they pursue and strive for in life.

My Child,

I really let you down. I am so sorry for not being there to hold your hand and show you the way in this crazy world that we live in. I am so sorry that I never picked up the phone to see how you were doing in school and make sure you were okay from day to day.

I'm so sorry your mom and I didn't work out. I am so sorry you had to cry yourself to sleep at night blaming yourself for my absence, thinking it was your fault that I wasn't in your life, and not knowing that I was just not ready to grow up and step up to be the parent you needed. I apologize from the depths of my heart for missing every important moment in your life.

Not being able to wish you well as you took off to do things I should have been there for… not being able to provide a dime… My child, I am so sorry. I can't take back how it all made you feel, but I do hope you accept my apology as I want you to be well and know that regardless of my immature ways, I love you and am downright proud of you.

Sincerely,
The Dad You Needed

The first time I knew I really had to forgive someone was in my teenage years. I had grown to really hate my earthly father. My mom and he had me at a very young age, so I get it—it's not exactly what you are prepared for at the ages of 16 and 19, but then again, you can still be some type of parent…right?

Growing up and seeing most kids at school during special events with both their parents around made me really wonder and think something was wrong with me. No one explained to me why my father wasn't around. I also didn't really know how to ask or communicate my curiosity either. I used to think and assume it was my fault that he wasn't in my life, thinking it was something I did or didn't do. I was tormented with thoughts that I wasn't good enough to have a father, or I wasn't worth loving. So I grew mad and angry at him for not coming around and being there for me. Not only did I hate him but I began to hate myself. I didn't like who I was, and I kept blaming myself for why he never came around.

His sister was a really great aunt to me. She knew

he wasn't a good father, but she still wanted to be a part of and make a difference in my life, and I am truly grateful for that. I remember one day when I was over at his sister's house, he happened to be there for a very short period. Upon leaving, he asked me if I could drive him to the store. I immediately said, "No." He asked me again, and I again said, "No! You have never done anything for me!" Plus, I knew all he wanted was a beer, and I really didn't want to support the life of addiction that he lived. He started getting mad at me and went to tell my aunt that he couldn't believe I said no. She then called me to the back where she was doing her hair in the master bathroom and said, "Bridgette, no matter what—he is still your father." In my young teenage mind, I couldn't believe she was taking up for him and about to make me do this with the guilt trip. Needless to say, I took him and dropped him off at my grandmother's house.

When jail was his second home, I managed to write to him there and let him know how hurt I was that he was never in my life and that I finally forgave him. The Lord had placed it on my heart too often for me to ignore what had to be done. Surprisingly, he wrote me back. Although that was the first and last time I had ever felt seen and acknowledged by my dad, it felt pretty good seeing as though I knew he had nothing but time to think about every word I wrote with no distractions and a sober mind.

The only time I would see my dad was around holidays when he would decide to come over to my grandmother's or aunt's house. Even then, it would never be a good memory. He was always drunk, starting drama, causing fights, and the next thing I knew, cops would be there. It never failed; it was always something with him during a holiday—if not a holiday then just a typical weekend when he would come by and ask my grandmother or aunt for money or a ride somewhere. Even as an adult with a family of my own, he still found a way to embarrass and disappoint me with how terribly he acted while drunk in front of my husband and kids during Thanksgiving. He tried to pick a fight with my husband, but I would not tolerate disrespect, and neither would my husband. The reason and randomness of it all was so silly; I honestly cannot even remember how the situation spiraled to that point. Nevertheless, my husband stood his ground being firm with respect for me as his wife and my grandmother's home, and then my dad just left as he slammed the front door.

Although my father is still absent in my life, I forgive him for that and every other moment of disappointment I've had to swallow. Forgiving him helped me to toss out the self-condemnation and self-hatred from all those years that I thought his absence was my fault. It brought me to a place of self-acceptance and peace in my heart that is really indescribable. It no longer bothers me that he is unwilling to change. How so? I have accepted that he has internal, deep-rooted battles that he has to deal with, and he is who he is until he desires a change for himself. No matter what, I will continue to pray for him. As my aunt said to me growing up—he is still my father.

2: Forgiving Your Spouse

It is so important for marriages to have a strong foundation in Christ, honor their wedding vows, and to glorify the Lord in all things. Marriage is hard work regardless of your religious beliefs. It is much harder when your Christian morals have been questioned, and you've given the enemy legal access to your marriage.

Dear Love of my Life,

I apologize for taking our vows for granted. Baby, I am so sorry that I thought it was okay to emotionally entertain another person. My heart aches knowing that it is my fault that your trust was broken and taken for granted.

Baby, I am so sorry that your heart was ripped out of your chest right underneath your nose. I am so sorry that, ever since then, you've had to deal with more insecurities than you've ever had before.

Words can't express how sorry I am for making you even have to question or doubt my loyalty and trust. I pray, in Jesus' name, that as we get through this together, every soul wound will be healed and delivered from each hurt and pain I have caused. I love you and will never disrespect you or our family ever again.

Sincerely,
The Luckiest Spouse Ever

Two months after I had gotten married, I was already questioning if I should leave the man to whom I had just said "for better or worse." I was already questioning if I should walk away from what I thought would be forever. I was already asking God, "Why?" I had already been going through a lot of heavy spiritual warfare, but now this was too much!

Learning that a woman from my husband's past was trying to immediately break our union because she didn't want to let go became a nightmare. She would randomly text him inappropriate messages. She even tried to shoot her best shot by purchasing an airline ticket for them to travel outside the state! That was extremely mortifying for me to find as the Lord led me to learn about all that had been hidden from me. As I was witnessing her name in a couple of emails and texts, my heart sank to its lowest, and I literally started shaking, trembling as I couldn't believe this was really happening to me.

I started thinking of so many things simultaneously.

Is he really doing this? What else has he been hiding? Is he seeing this chick? Why would he take my trust for granted and do this to me? Does our marriage and family mean anything to him? Along with so many questions and thoughts shaking me up, I started trying to make sense of why he had been acting differently. He had been more irritable, and it didn't take much for him to get mad and blame things on me. We'd been arguing all the time lately. It made sense why I had been dreaming about people from our past.

At that point, I knew it was time to start praying against the enemy and for soul ties from both of our pasts to be broken. Was it easy to immediately jump right into prayer? No—not at all. According to Proverbs 11:14, "Where no counsel is, the people fall; but in the multitude of counselors there is safety." I most certainly had to call on counsel because I knew I couldn't be in my flesh, feelings, or rely on my own thought process. I love my husband, but I love God more, so I had to also kneel before the Lord alone and truly ask Him what I should do as I only wanted to be led by the Holy Spirit, giving God all the glory in the matter. There in that secret place, God reminded me of the time he revealed to us our purpose together, especially as his wife.

When you have a God-given purpose in your marriage, the enemy will use individuals (especially the weak and small-minded) to do whatever they can do to break and divide your divine marital covenant with God, but rest assured that if you stay close to God through it all, he will stay close to you and get you through. Although my husband had not physically cheated on me, it still hurt that he gave another woman his time, leading her emotions to grow a bigger pool of false hope imagining things about them and what could potentially still be as they continued to text. Staying in God's word and his presence allowed me to remain by my husband's side, get through, and forgive him for foolishly entertaining a woman he had no intentions on ever seeing again.

Was it simple? Heck no! If I can be honest, the old me and my flesh was saying, "Leave him and move on." The old me and my flesh was saying, "Girl, you know we have never taken any crap from a man, and we won't start now!" However, when you truly ask the Lord to have his way with your heart, emotions, and perspective, He will do just that. I then chose to think about how we were both very new to "the married life" and accepted that it would take time for us to truly grow and mature in being husband and wife.

I chose to think about the word of God in 1 Corinthians 13:4-8 that says, "Love is patient, love is kind. It does not envy, it does not boast, it is not proud. It does not dishonor others, it is not self seeking, it is not easily angered, it keeps no records of wrongs. Love does not delight in evil but rejoices with the truth. It always protects, always trusts, always hopes, always preserves. Love never fails. But where there are prophecies, they will cease; where there are tongues, they will be stilled; where there is knowledge, it will pass away."

I stood on the word of God in James 1:2-5 that says, "Consider it pure joy, my brothers and sisters, whenever you face trials of many kinds, because you know that the testing of your faith produces perseverance. Let perseverance finish its work so that you may be mature and complete, not lacking anything." I believed then and I still believe now that God is going to honor his word to us as we continually stand on it.

The danger of not forgiving can grow weeds of so

much bitterness, strife, and unwanted chaos from roots of insecurities. The same nagging conversations come up that can end in a fight, leading to possible days of no talking and no peace in the home. The same tormenting negative thoughts can taunt you, consume your heart, and play with your imagination leading to possible suspicion or accusations (all lies from the enemy). Sometimes, it can even be subconsciously easier to believe the lies of the enemy in the mind rather than what has already been discussed between you and your spouse just because you've already chosen not to forgive and release yourself from such burden. The word of God says in Mark 3:25, "If a house is divided against itself, that house cannot stand." The friction derived from unforgiveness is very unhealthy for you and your children and could lead to a very unhappy home or worse—a divided home.

While seeking counseling is a great option, if both aren't willing to be vulnerable and speak their truth with an open heart to forgive then counseling could be ineffective. It has helped my husband and I both to come to that place of vulnerability where God had more to work with and was able to really get the glory out of our willingness to fully forgive each other and heal.

Ephesians 4:32 says, "Be kind and compassionate to one another, forgiving each other, just as in Christ God forgave you." Forgiving my husband with grace and mercy has been a great blessing to us both. My husband feels it has impacted us in a positive way because it allowed us to heal, grow, and mature. He also feels that it takes time and maturity to understand what you really want out of marriage, and I totally agree, as it has truly made us stronger. The space he was in mentally is far from where he is today. He has evolved in so many ways, and I'm thankful that I continued to walk by faith and not by sight, holding onto the promises of God and every prophetic word that was spoken over us from His prophets. I see a lot of marriages tossed away so quickly due to not being rooted in Christ and because of the lack of prayer, patience, communication, and discernment, or by the influence of others. The only influence on your marriage should be our Heavenly Father, Jesus Christ, and the Holy Spirit.

3: Forgiving A Sibling

Having a sibling is truly special, and I know because I have five. You know that a relationship is special when you have a bond that is based on a transparency where you can talk about anything and just be who you are with no worries or fears of being judged and rejected. Not in all but in most cases, having a sibling teaches one how to be a friend, how to love, how to share, how to care, and how to be there for someone besides oneself. Access to trust and the heart is given immediately from birth until proven otherwise, and that is something never to take for granted and always cherish—no matter the age.

Dear Sib,

I am so sorry for hurting you by pushing you away when I was going through life's ups and downs. I am so sorry for bringing you to tears, piercing your heart when I stopped answering your calls, and ignoring your texts when you just wanted to connect and help.

I truly apologize for betraying you when you put yourself on the line for me and abusing your trust. I am so sorry for getting offended and not accepting how God made you to speak your truth, being boldly vocal and expressive. I apologize for choosing new friends over you when you've been my best friend, my bodyguard, and my biggest fan from day one.

A lot of people have failed me, but you've always been there for me. I am sincerely apologetic for judging your imperfections with a critical eye because of what others said and thought about you. I had no right to condemn, judge, and look down on you because you had a baby out of wedlock. I unconditionally love you and your babies no matter how they came into this world.

Sincerely,
Your First Best Friend

For some of us, life can be a scary ride or a big adventure when you're first coming out of high school or college. There was a time in one of my siblings' lives where they were really trying to find themselves, and unfortunately during that same period, the enemy tried to destroy our relationship.

It was tough and heartbreaking to suddenly feel like a stranger or rather an enemy to someone you love so much and to whom you have always been seemingly close. The deception the enemy had them under regarding me and other parts of their life troubled my heart tremendously—and my pocket, financially. You see, being pregnant and having to travel out of state to clean out an apartment you co-signed for, make arrangements for furniture to be picked up and for lease termination, and pay for unplanned months of rent due to a selfish decision your sibling made abruptly can be very troublesome and a huge bitter pill to swallow when you're held liable.

The circle of friends my sibling chose to keep close

would strangely condemn me for my flaws and weaknesses. Did they know me? No, but they assumed a lot for whatever reason and would use my sibling to try and get money from me or to charge spiritual attacks at me. Regardless of how harsh and distant my sibling started treating me, I never stopped loving and praying for them. I never gave up on them. I never counted them out. Every time the Holy Spirit would speak to me about them, I'd immediately go into prayer and follow as led to do whatever next. I kept the fight of faith knowing that the bible in Ephesians 6:12 says, "For we wrestle not against flesh and blood, but against principalities, against powers, against the rulers of darkness of this world, against spiritual wickedness in high places." When you know your word, and you know that it's deeper than what is on the surface of one's behavior, but most importantly that this is a spirit that you're dealing with, then it's easier to NOT throw in the towel and give up on that person or relationship.

With that being said, I had to get out of my emotions and remember my authority in Christ Jesus. I kept praying and declaring their deliverance daily, for the prayers of the righteous person are powerful and effective. I also had to remember that I, too, was once lost but now found by a God who will never let me go. If he did it for me, he would do it for them for "the righteous person may have many troubles, but the Lord delivers him from them all," according to Psalms 34:19. Psalms 37:24 also reminds us that "though he may stumble, he will not fall, for the Lord upholds him with his hand."

After eight months of waiting patiently on the Lord's timing, he delivered and brought my sibling back to my family and me. The second greatest command of God is to love thy neighbor as thyself, and so, although my trust wasn't where it used to be, I chose to forgive and help them get back on their feet. Colossians 3:13 says, "forbearing one another, and forgiving one another, if any man have a quarrel against any: even as Christ forgave you, so also do ye."

Forgiving my sibling was the best thing I did for myself and for our family. As we are both perfectly imperfect, with time, we are closer than we have ever been. We have rebuilt our trust in certain areas and are still working on the others which is truly ok with both of us, as we are on our own pace—naturally, as we are led by the Holy Spirit. My children are absolutely crazy about them. They look up to my sibling and simply adore spending time with them, and the feelings are mutual. They have such a blessed and beautiful bond.

It is amazing what God can do when you do your part and let God do His! I realized that when you have a loved one that you're extremely concerned about, the best thing to do is to truly give them to God, always pray for and love them—even if it's from afar. It's not about you controlling the situation to get everything the way you feel their life should be. It's not about getting through to them and fulfilling your plans and vision for their life. You are not Lord of their life or soul. Fighting for their soul spiritually through constantly interceding is more powerful and effective than arguing with someone or entertaining a matter that only God can change.

4: Forgiving A Work Colleague

In a workplace, there should always be respect, boundaries, a positive environment, and a collaborative team effort to meet the company's short- and long-term goals. Some may have their own professional/individual goals, which is fine as long as it doesn't affect others in a negative way. I personally like to work in peace while getting along with everyone but without feeling like I have to look over my shoulder every five minutes.

Dear Fellow Colleague,

I apologize to you for making you uncomfortable, always finding fault in you with a critical eye. I truly apologize for being so pushy and for the way I went about embarrassing you and putting you on the spot in front of our colleagues. I should have backed off after another colleague interjected and offered to do the task needed at hand. I also apologize for constantly judging you. A lot of times, there is nothing wrong with what you do; it's just not the way I would do it. I have a bad habit of always wanting to be in control, and I feel terrible for always picking on you for self-gratification.

I am also terribly sorry for the way I attacked and brought defamation to your character to management. I completely threw you under the bus for something you didn't even do or say. I should have heard your side of the story first before making accusations. It was very poor judgment and it should have never gotten that far. I apologize for not appreciating and overlooking how much you bring to our company. At the time, I may have gotten so caught up on trying to shine and show management that I was ready for my own management position that I was willing to make you look bad at all costs.

Sincerely,
The Pessimistic Problem Seeker

There are those colleagues that are cool to do small talk with, but you keep your distance. There may be one who brings life to the party every day, and you thank God for them because you don't know how you'd make it weekly if it were not for the positive and fun vibes he or she brings. There are a couple of colleagues who are always serious, and you just say "hey" and "bye" in passing. There is always that one who you know you can't trust as far as you can throw them because they feed off of drama and like to keep a good gossiping session around. Since that is the case, you definitely know to keep them at bay. You have one or two with whom you can always pray and share your family high and low seasons.

Then there's the one who some like to call the "brown-noser." Between this colleague and the one who likes to gossip, you have to literally make a conscious effort to keep them at bay and watch everything you say. The "brown-noser" is the type of person who, no matter what or how you say something, is looking for something to make out of nothing to get attention from management and make themselves look like they saved the day.

Usually, I was good about keeping individuals with certain bad spirit/negative characteristics at a distance to protect my peace, but this particular colleague (a "brown-noser") had a nice family, and their spouse and kids would always come over and speak to me. Since our kids were the same age, it was always easy and nice to greet and show them love, as they always reminded me of my own.

One morning out of nowhere, the Lord gave me a dream about them. It was very brief but made me concerned. I, of course, immediately prayed for them after waking up. A few days later when I saw that colleague, I asked how his family was doing, and he said they were fine. I mentioned a part of my dream to them, and they just reiterated that the family was well. I continued to pray because I rarely get dreams about colleagues, and in the case that I do, I can't take it lightly. Going on about my business, I learned a few days later that the colleague had a family member that recently passed away. I was so heartbroken to hear the news, so I offered to get a card on behalf of the staff to have everyone sign for moral support.

I continuously kept them lifted as everyone did, I'm sure. A few weeks later, a very rude client came on the scene and was nasty and downright hateful to everyone including myself. The client was extremely rude even to the other clients who were around; I only know that part because they expressed their concerns and comments. I thought I handled the client well by "killing her with kindness," keeping it short and sweet as they were not only rude but also confused. I expressed specifically how we could help her and in the end told her to have a blessed day.

My colleague called me to his office and expressed to me privately that he didn't like that I stated what our clients typically do in order to have an effective and successful experience. While I respected his opinion, I explained the entire situation to help him understand why I had to explain proper protocol to the client. Not long after that matter (that I thought was over), I then was contacted by management about the entire situation. Management expressed to me what the colleague said (to more than one manager), and my colleague basically made me out to be some type of rude, obnoxious villain. Management knew that wasn't my character and had worked with me longer than the colleague to know that wasn't true—so I was grateful for that. I confronted the colleague about it immediately, and the colleague tried to downplay the seriousness of the matter and lie about what was said to management so that I wouldn't be upset.

I was confused in more than one way, and I know confusion is not of God, so I knew immediately who the colleague was being used by, especially when stirring up trouble to management and giving false allegations became so easy. I can't lie and say I was not hurt. I was hurt because, out of all my colleagues, I didn't expect for this one to ever attack my character to management or anyone's for that matter. Although at times they had a bad tendency of being a "brown-noser," I gave them the benefit of doubt since I had so much respect for their family and enjoyed occasionally speaking with their spouse.

Which leads me to the next reason I was hurt… I felt I had lost a potential friend in Christ—not with the colleague but their spouse. We were developing a good relationship over time by checking in with each other via text and small talk whenever they came by the workplace. I genuinely liked their spouse and was in high hopes to one day get our kids together for potential play dates. Hurt had a way of sinking in as I couldn't understand why the colleague felt the need to discuss me with management since we had already privately and respectfully talked about the matter in their office. It also hurt because I had been privately interceding for their family as I had more dreams about them after the first one.

One of the ministers in my church (a small group I was in at the time) told me to continue praying for them after it was my turn to share certain things in my heart. I shared with them that I was hurt about that situation and that I also needed strength to not be in my flesh at work but to continue to be led by the spirit of the Lord. I felt that, even after that unnecessary incident, this colleague would always find their way to try and make "something out of nothing" with me. It was hard to just have a natural and genuine work dynamic around them.

I had NEVER had to deal with this at a workplace

before. Have you ever worked with anyone like that before? I mean, it really became a nuisance because they just wouldn't stay in their lane and know their place due to their intense desire to be a manager themselves. It became rather clear to me that they could not be trusted. They were always super inquisitive with the wrong motives. It got to the point where I was no longer comfortable around them alone.

Matthews 6:14-15 says, "For if you forgive other people when they sin against you, your heavenly Father will also forgive you. But if you do not forgive others their sins, your Father will not forgive your sins." I eventually forgave that colleague. It wasn't easy to do overnight—that is for sure.

The bible also says in Matthew 5:44, "But I tell you, love your enemies and pray for those who persecute you," and Psalm 119:1-3 says, "Blessed are those whose ways are blameless, who walk according to the law of the Lord. Blessed are those who keep his statutes and seek him with all their heart—they do no wrong but follow his ways."

Working with difficult personalities can be very challenging because you see them forty hours a week or more, and if the atmosphere consumes strife and other bad spirits, it can be more stressful and sometimes the main reason why a workplace has high turnovers.

It's important to seek the Lord and pray diligently to get to that point of forgiveness. Though it can be extremely hard, when one's character is lied about or if one is constantly being judged by a person who has a critical spirit, having a diligent prayer life with God will release that very one from this world of emotions and grudges one would naturally find easy to cling to by fleshly or carnal ways.

The more I prayed for God to help me to release the offense, I was able to see the colleague like Chist and forgave. I started thinking about the part of their life that I don't know. The battles, the mountains, and the defeated moments they may have experienced—portions of their life that make them feel like they have to do whatever it takes to get to the top or to feel validated by man.

Luke 6:35 says, "But love your enemies, do good to them, and lend to them without expecting to get anything back. Then your reward will be great, and you will be children of the Most High, because he is kind to the ungrateful and wicked." I was also reminded in prayer and through his word that, while it's not an excuse, no one is as perfect as God, and everyone is not as strong in the Lord as others, so we have to continue to be kind, giving each other grace and mercy.

5: Forgiving An Opportunist Disguised As A Friend

Having a childhood friend who goes with you through life can be very comforting when facing new seasons that can often be scary at the beginning. Traveling to big cities, climbing new heights together, and having the feeling of someone familiar by your side through it all can be rather exciting... unless things change.

Dear Friend-Foe,

I apologize for misleading you about our friendship and using you for my own personal gains in life. I should have been upfront, but I didn't know how to tell you I was still mad at you and holding onto childhood grudges. I'm sorry I couldn't be vulnerable around you.

I'm sorry I couldn't be the genuine and trustworthy friend you expected me to be. I apologize for constantly dragging all my baggage, problems, and struggles into your life for you to fix with no intention of genuinely being there for you if you needed the same. I regret and sincerely apologize for allowing my insecurities to cause more division and discord between us.

I'm so sorry for hurting you by putting more effort into being spiteful and vindictive than thoughtful and unselfish. Regardless of how I feel toward you, you were always there for me, and I am truly sorry I couldn't be there to show kindhearted, genuine moral support with unconditional love when you really needed me the most.

Sincerely,
The Benefit of the Doubt

I knew a young lady ever since second grade. We would read books together on the school bus and talk during those long rides on the back country roads to and from school. We ended up being in school together from elementary to college. We didn't really become close until high school. We went to high school football and basketball games together as she didn't live far from our high school. I would sleep over at her house at times, and we would do each other's hair or talk on the phone with guys we had no business talking to. We told each other just about everything. Her mom had a great, down to earth, and sweet spirit with a beautiful smile. She was very fond of me and likewise with my mom towards my friend. Her mom was a hair stylist and would even trim or color my hair with blonde streaks at her shop. She was the only stylist I was comfortable with doing my hair, and it was an added plus that I enjoyed being there with her and my friend after school. I began to look at her like a sister and really enjoyed the bond we were forming.

Although we hit a bump in the road with our friendship during our senior year of high school, I didn't give up on us getting through it. A mutual friend who cared and was concerned about us not talking played a key part in the initial reconciling phase. Her mom was also hopeful that we would reconcile; we had a good conversation one day when I called her house, and she mentioned her thoughts to me.

Prior to going to college, I helped her with information about the school that had already accepted me since she was having a few issues with her initial choice. We wound up going to the same college as well as a few other girls with whom we went to high school. Even though we hung around the same girls from back at home, I would always notice how she would seem standoffish and like she didn't want to say much. I didn't know if it was because of something at home she didn't want to talk about, if she was homesick, or if it was because of financial aid issues she didn't want to mention. I didn't want to pry, so I wouldn't say much but would still be there for her by offering her a ride when I was driving off campus to go to different places since I was the only one from our hometown who had a car on campus.

I saw her like a sister, and being there for her was never a question until I started picking up on some back-stabbing signs from her. She started forming patterns as if she was always out for herself and never as considerate of me as I was for her. When I found out that I was immediately moving to Washington, DC after graduating college, as I had accepted a television entertainment position—a dream-come-true job of mine—she was not happy for me at all and seemed extremely sulky about it. I was so thrilled my hard work as a summer intern in NY had paid off, but her disposition came off as rather jealous. I'm not sure if it was because she had the honor cords and I didn't, and she felt as if she should have received a call before I did, or if it was because she just couldn't be happy for me since she wasn't happy with herself. I would have liked to have thought the second reason, however when I saw how happy she was about our mutual friend also receiving a new job, it was clear to me that it was a personal issue towards me.

After relocating and starting my new job, I learned that she still hadn't gotten a call back for any jobs. After much prayer, I came up with a plan to get her an internship at my job since I knew one of our departments really needed help. I felt in my spirit that once they got a good vibe and sensed the type of person she was, they would eventually hire her. She came up to Maryland to stay with me at my apartment, and I initially allowed her however much time she needed to get on her feet. Not even two weeks after staying with me, she was on the phone talking behind my back about me and something petty she was not happy with. I was shocked because I welcomed her into my home and also into my workplace, and that was how she chose to show her appreciation. After she apologized, I forgave her and tried to move on per usual.

She finally got hired, and I was thrilled for not only such an opportunity that had finally opened up for her but also because four months of letting her live with me rent-free, driving her to work, and paying for a lot of dinners started taking a toll on my pocket, and my heart, as the backbiting continued. After she got to where she wanted to be, when I needed her the most—during my lowest point in life as a single woman—she would treat me like crap, as if I had never done a thing to help her. She would do catty things just to be mean, leaving and sneaking out of the office early without mentioning it so I wouldn't ask to go out to eat with her. In the mornings, she would purposely leave her dirty underwear on the bathroom floor knowing that I would at some point have to use the toilet and get ready for work. It was as if she was trying to intentionally provoke me, but I prayed up and continued to seek God on my next move. I had even rededicated my life to Christ during such a season, not allowing the mischief to keep me away from Him and refusing to stoop to such levels.

God knows I tried to be there for her through our life, but our ties to each other had apparently overextended their stay. We were just two different people with two different hearts. I have never been the type to want to compete, tear someone down, or be selfish, and it just wasn't a good fit or a good idea to keep her in my life. She clearly didn't have the eyes to see me nor the heart to love me as God gave me for her.

All of this really made my heart heavy, and I wanted closure and peace, so I called and asked her why she did all those hurtful things to me. How could you treat someone you've known for so long that way and not be bothered? Do you feel like you betrayed me? Her response was, "Time doesn't mean anything with friendships… every situation you mentioned has been the furthest from my mind… Although I'm very grateful for what you've done, I think you feel I owe you something… I admit that I had some catty stuff going on, and I agree that it was a lack of effort. Something just wouldn't allow me to get close to you—don't get close to Bridgette."

I was stunned at the response. It wasn't about her owing me anything. It was about her valuing our friendship and not using me. When anyone is sincerely grateful, you know it, whether they pay you back or not. It blew me away that it never even crossed her mind to show common courtesy, love, and respect towards me.

I was mad at myself for a moment for not accepting the red flags as they revealed themselves more. I kept trying to give her the benefit of the doubt since I had known her for so long, but I guess she was right about one thing: time doesn't mean anything, especially for those you have outgrown or who have outgrown you.

Looking back on things, I truly believe in my spirit

that she never let go of the bump we ran into back in high school. I forgave her for her wrongdoing, but I believe she never forgave me for mine, and no relationship can thrive or survive like that. I was sincerely apologetic, and I had expressed that. Had I known she was just on a joyride to get whatever opportunities she could snatch while around me, I would have cut ties with her a lot sooner. Of course, she knew that which is why, seven years after high school, she failed to mention to me "that something told her not to get close to me."

It hurt to learn this, but the conversation that brought closure and helped cut the ties of friendship was much needed so that I could be free with no resentment, grudges, or burdens on my heart. Did it happen immediately? No way, but the moment I knew I was truly free from it was when it didn't bother me to hear her name or have to converse with her during certain work hours. God granted me favor with the television company for eight years, and while I was still there, there were assignments I still had to communicate with her about. She may have still felt some type of way about me, but God healed my heart, and I am truly grateful.

If it had not been for that experience, I wouldn't be

as wise and sharp as I am today. Since then, God has truly blessed me with double for my trouble as I only aim to please him. When we treat people poorly, it says more about us than it does them, and we all will have to answer to God as we are accountable for our own salvation. Mark 12:31 says, "The second is this: 'Love your neighbor as yourself.' There is no commandment greater than these." I pray that as tough as it may be, you always pray to God to help you to do the right thing and treat people the way you want to be treated. Someone may have to give you more grace and mercy one day and vice versa. Choose to listen and obey God, and he will always honor you with favor when you do.

6: Forgiving A Mother-In-Law

A role of a mother-in-law can be a special and beautiful addition to your life or a wicked nightmare that won't seem to go away. She can bless you by being there with open arms and a big nurturing heart to love your family unconditionally, or she can curse you by the negative words of venom she speaks as she constantly rejects you rather than accepts you. She can adjust to you being the new King or Queen taking priority in her child's new life, or she can always have the mindset that everything is and should always remain about her. While offering opinions without passing judgment and with a nurturing spirit, she can respect your parenting style, or she can suggest things offensively with the motive and intent to take over by forcing her ways upon you and completely negating your views. It is extremely important for a mother-in-law to know her place with healthy boundaries set so that it doesn't affect the marriage or relationships with present or future grandchildren.

Dear In-Law,

I am truly apologetic regarding how I've treated you and made you feel since you've been in my child's (your spouse's) life. I am so sorry for never accepting and embracing you into our family with unconditional loving arms. I am sorry for all the boundaries I've overstepped by my actions and my choice of words. To be honest, bridling my tongue has always been a weakness of mine, and I am truly sorry for saying the things I should have never said. I apologize deeply for saying disrespectful things about you around your children (our grandchildren). I've been praying for the Lord to help me with that for some time now, and although I have faith He will, it's something I too have to really desire for myself and start being intentional with.

I'm sorry for always coming down on you about things you should or should not do, when at times, I don't even take my own advice. I realize I have passed a lot of judgment about how you all choose to raise your children. I truly apologize for taking over all the time. Many times, I should have stepped back and respected how you felt with intentions to understand as I listened without being so quick to immediately dismiss why you chose to make the decisions you made, and still make, in your own household. I also apologize for caring more about what people think and allowing it to affect our relationship, allowing pride and self-righteous thinking to be the driving force of our relationship. As parents who are still trying to find your way, I'm so sorry for not being there when you all needed me the most. I know parenthood is not always easy. We were so blessed and fortunate to have help back when we had young children, and I have to sadly admit that we have not been there for you in the same way. I am so sorry for being so wrapped up and entangled with myself that I forgot how to relate, empathize, and love you through. I'm so sorry for only being around when it is mainly convenient or beneficial for me in the end. I am so sorry for not building a healthy, safe, trustworthy, and comfortable foundation for you to be able to easily come to me anytime you may feel you need help.

As I look back on things that I wish I could have done differently, I could have been there more for you after you had our grandchildren. I could have come over so you could catch up on some sleep when your children were newborns. I could have brought over some nice, home-cooked food during your first couple of weeks of maternity leave when you couldn't do much but breastfeed and make sure the babies were happy. I am so sorry for not calling to see if you needed anything from the store while I was out during the moments you were home alone with the babies, as I know your immediate family is hours away from where you stay. I am so sorry for never even taking the time to celebrate you as a parent. Our grandchildren are crazy about you, and they have every right to be. I know deep down that you are doing the very best that you can with the strength of the Lord.

I am truly regretful of how I tried to use your own flesh and blood against you. Family is so important, and I am so sorry for constantly putting my child between us, forcing them to always have to mediate and juggle the value of each personal view in order to keep the peace. I truly apologize for not treating you right from the beginning and receiving your love when all you've ever done was try to embrace our family, try to bring us closer to our child, and try to be a part of our world. I know it is not right to be moody towards you, and I will work on being more loving like Christ. You've been the best thing for my child and a blessing to the family. I've taken all these years for granted not truly getting to know who you really are above the surface. I am truly regretful and sorry for disappointing you by bringing so much painful rejection and hurtful judgment upon you. I pray God will help us mend our relationship and truly get the glory with restoration from all the moments lost.

Sincerely,
The Nurturing Support You Pray For

When one has been through so much due to consuming unhealthy and toxic relationships, it becomes mentally draining. Trying to be a people pleaser in efforts to gain acceptance and to prove to people that you are in fact who God says you are is constantly frustrating, depressing, and very destructive to one's well-being. It's even more painful and exhausting when those same people are members of your family, especially when it's a family member to whom you have never done any harm, to whom you'd never thought you would have to convince of your innocence, and to whom you never dreamt you'd have to prove your love.

Unfortunately, that was my life with an in-law that I love but with whom I found it extremely hard to have a healthy and genuine relationship. Amongst other hard life matters that I had to get through, this relationship caused a different type of heartache. Every time I got to a point where my emotional wound would come to a place of total healing, soon after, another scar, punch, or jab came, and it was back to square one again. Each new time would feel like a bigger scar or bruise that took longer to heal and recover from.

Now, you may laugh when you read this, but I seriously feel like I forgave this relative just like the bible says in Matthew 18:22, "seventy-seven times"—if not more. Ha! Now, nothing is wrong with that because I know we all fall short of the glory of God, and God's command is to be obeyed. However, I just didn't expect it to be this way with this person and as frequent. Out of all things, this was something I'd never thought I'd even have to pray about so much. Forgiving and seeking God on how we could really reconcile this time or reconcile another time started to become a part of my life journey with this relative, as I was always seeking to please God and have a pure heart. At one point, it had gotten so stressful that I was led by the Lord to even practice what the bible says in Matthew 18:15-16: "If your brother or sister sins, go and point out their fault, just between the two of you. If they listen to you, you have won them over. But if they will not listen, take one or two others along, so that 'every matter may be established by the testimony of two or three witnesses." I always hoped that our desires for our relationship would be the same (for the sake of our family) and that one day we could look back and laugh at all the ridiculous stories the enemy tried to plot against us.

For me, one of the biggest challenges in forgiving this relative was when my husband and I humbly considered temporarily staying with them for a few months while we were transitioning from selling a home to buying another home and were denied that as an option. During that transition, there was a period when we were literally homeless for a few months and had to stay with my sister in her third-floor, one-bedroom apartment on her pull-out sofa. We then spent a couple of weeks at our children's Godparents' house, all while I was pregnant with our youngest.

Talk about hard times, right? Although we had been staying at a temporary apartment we had leased and planned to be there through the entire lease or until our new house was finished (as it was a new construction home), a few things occurred to me while staying on the apartment property that made us feel uncomfortable, unsafe, and undervalued as tenants. The last straw was when my husband's vehicle was broken into and when my car was completely stolen. The way management handled that entire situation was unethical and unacceptable. Mind you, I was VERY much pregnant and should not have been at all stressed out on the level I was. With all the prior issues we had living there, after that, we knew we had to leave and find somewhere else to stay for peace and sanity to protect our family and to avoid having my baby girl prematurely.

I was extremely hurt by the word curses of shame, judgment and rejection that went forth behind our backs and for many other reasons. Due to the word of God that says in 1 Timothy 5:8, "Anyone who does not provide for their relatives, and especially for their own household, has denied the faith and is worse than an unbeliever." I had great hope that we could count on being helped and loved through such delicate times, that it would not be an issue to lay our heads somewhere we could feel safe for just a few months. It wasn't as if we did not have a plan or as if we were irresponsible adults who had a hidden agenda. With common ground rules and an agreed upon exit date in place, I had even allowed friends and family to stay with me plenty of times to get themselves on their feet and thought it was something all Christians did to help each other whether you were family or not.

Although my relationship with this relative wasn't always peachy, as I humbled myself to consider living with them, I also found myself becoming optimistic at how this moment that the enemy meant for evil, God could work out for our good by bringing us closer together and allowing us to bond before our youngest joined as the new addition to our family. While I started thinking about the good that could come out of this rather than the worst that could possibly happen, that wasn't the case on the other end.

That cut ran deep because, despite our past differences, I thought we could lay our present differences aside for the sake of our children. We love our children so much and would do anything for them no matter what. If it wasn't about me or my husband, it should have surely been considered even more for our children, especially the one who was still in my belly waiting to arrive and meet everyone. I had been let down before but never like this. Seeing my husband so disappointed, rejected, and hurt just as much if not worse was not easy to witness either. Talk about kicking a man while he is down… and from your own family. The enemy was up to no good, per usual, stirring up more deception, lies, and confusion. This led us to choose to protect our family's peace at all costs by staying where we were welcomed, safe, and loved unconditionally.

My husband and I are so much stronger and wiser, although it hurt severely to learn how the relative really devalued me and would rather see me down than up, especially if it inconvenienced them. If I can be honest, I wanted to cut them out of my life immediately and effectively before I had our daughter, but spending time with God helped me to get past my feelings and forgive. The relative and I have since seen each other many times at family gatherings and talked, as I have chosen to forgive and continue to walk in love. Just like God worked all things out for Joseph when his brothers betrayed him, God worked all things out for us, too. If it were not for the rejection, my husband would have never felt like his back was up against the wall, forcing him to step up at the most vulnerable time of his life to do whatever needed to be done to take care of his family and to never have to worry about asking another person for anything.

The persecution and rejection set off a new spark and zeal to find new passions that were lying within him the entire time, and he is now very successful in all. Hallelujah, thank you Jesus! God's plans and provision for our life didn't come how we expected, but they came to pass how he saw fit—for his glory and for our good (Romans 8:28). Being abandoned challenged and forced us out of our traditional comfort zone that led us on a new journey of finding our new church home where we love and serve. When times were really hard, it gave us a desire to stay close to God and stay accountable with like-minded believers under a safe covering where our entire family is fed, nurtured, and fruitful.

Our marriage has been strengthened from withstanding a loved one with toxic tendencies. I've literally seen a relationship that ended due to a potential in-law with a bullying spirit causing strain on the relationship from such negativity and making one or the other feel as if they needed to choose peace at whatever cost, even if it cost them to break up. To this day, I often think about that couple and what their relationship would have been like had the potential in-law stayed in their lane with healthy boundaries.

No longer are we walking in fear or being controlled by manipulation, intimidation, or judgment.

No longer are we walking with our heads down, questioning our worth and value to man. No longer are we just allowing anyone to have access to our peace without healthy boundaries. No longer will the opinion of people DISTRACT, DESTROY, or DOWNPLAY our value nor DICTATE how we see ourselves. We didn't understand it then, but we understand it clearly now. It's so refreshing as God gets ALL the glory for changing our story.

Forgiving my in-law has truly freed me to the point where I am completely unbothered. I no longer lose sleep if I am dismissed or deliberately disrespected in my own home by unwanted criticism. My emotions are not controlled by the desire of needing to be accepted. Although certain things have not been accepted about me by them, I have accepted to continue to pray for their deliverance as it is not I who has to solve the problems, but it is the Lord who is in charge of the final mending of all fences. I always felt like I needed to find a way to make it right or constantly explain myself to be understood. Accepting that this battle is not mine—it is the Lord's—is even more freeing.

7: Forgiving Yourself

Since God made total forgiveness available through Jesus Christ for anyone who believes and accepts him as Lord, it is just as important to love and forgive yourself as you also forgive others in order to be free and no longer bound by sin and the past. Loving yourself is important and most effective when you know yourself. When you know yourself in Christ, it creates self-awareness and confidence no one can ever take from you, making it ten times harder for the enemy to bring self condemnation and strife to your life. Once I realized this, I wrote a love letter and apology to myself in the year of 2014.

Dear Self,

I hope this letter finds you in great spirits! Even if it doesn't, I pray it is able to uplift your spirits after reading. I want to first start off by saying I love you! You are truly amazing and an inspiration. I love the woman you are becoming. God has really blessed and transformed so many things about you! It is amazing to see. I know you've been through so much with people, family and just life, period. I understand that you may be dealing with hurt and/or healing from betrayal or lack of love from others, but know this: I LOVE YOU!

We're going to get through this and everything together. Trust me, and most of all, TRUST GOD! You're worthy to still have the very best and live life abundantly because Jesus' blood made you worthy. You're going to continue to rise above and excel in ways like never before. Don't worry about who wasn't there and/or who still isn't there. God is there, and He is ALL that matters.

I'm sorry for ever making you second guess yourself or doubt who you are. I am so sorry for being so hard on you and not knowing your worth and true value when it came to who you should date. I'm sincerely sorry for allowing the enemy to place you in bondage by opinions, approval, and rejection from others. That was not right, and I promise I am going to do better.

No longer will I allow the enemy to attack the being and purpose upon your life. I love, accept, and appreciate everything about you, and SO DOES GOD! He loves you and has so much in store for you. No longer will I allow you to base your identity upon what man thinks about you. You are justified, saved, forgiven, loved, unblemished, the apple of God's eye, one spirit with the Lord, and redeemed! You are God's child and a sister to Christ.

I pray that you forgive me for ever leading you astray and not loving you as I should have. You are perfectly imperfect and I LOVE YOU!

Sincerely,
The One Set Free

The spirit of the Lord instructed me to start writing love letters to myself for self-healing as I had been through so much and sometimes still struggle. Previously in 2014, when I was initially instructed to write the letter you just read, it helped release me from a lot of hurt people had caused and brought me to a new place with myself, as it was hard to see myself the way God saw me. I didn't love myself enough to place healthy boundaries from toxic people. I didn't see myself as worth respecting by making sure only positive people surrounded and poured into me. Had I had been more careful of who had access to me, I could have avoided a lot.

    Acknowledging and forgiving myself for that was vital to reaching a needed breakthrough. A lot of the hurt and rejection caused me depression that I hid from many. It was the type of depression that would cause me to even question my life. From that season, I learned that when depression tries to sneak in, literally stop where you are, kneel, and pray. For Psalms 34:17

says, "The righteous cry out, and the Lord hears them, he delivers them from ALL their troubles." I learned that it's okay to tune the world out so you can tune God in. Sometimes, there are just too many voices and when daily decisions have to be made; it's imperative to be sensitive to the Holy Spirit. 1 Chronicles 16:11 says to "Seek the Lord and his strength; seek his face continually." I disconnected not only from a lot of voices but from people and went through a few years of consecration.

I get judged a lot by those who think I am just "Mrs. Holy," "Mrs. Perfect," or "Mrs. Pretty," and I am far from that. Certain trials and tribulations bring forth a true need to be closer to God. I just had to change a lot of my ways and surrender to the Lord especially when I realized it was costing me peace. The bible instructs us in James 1:22 this: "But be ye doers of the word, and not hearers only, deceiving your own selves." I enjoyed singing and praying to God to help me be like Christ Jesus, but the moment a situation of hurt came up, I had to learn to put into practice what I was singing and praying for to God.

When tested or tempted, exercising the word of God not only helped me to resist being carnal-minded—a hypocritical Christian, but it helped me to start avoiding repeated life lessons, resisting the enemy, and drawing closer to Christ Jesus. I realized the more we are like him in forgiveness, love, patience, kindness, and all his ways, the more he can use us, trusting us with his secrets to do the works for his Kingdom.

It is only by the Lord's goodness, grace, and mercy that I have gotten closer to Him. I've repented, gone deeper within, and I've never been the same since because, at the end of the day, no one is worth your peace or salvation. Yes, the enemy tried to take me out but praise God I am still standing. When he tries to take you out, just laugh and give it to God. Submit to God. Resist the devil, and he will flee. May the God of peace crush Satan under your feet as I declare and decree the grace of our Lord is with you!

8: My Apology To You

According to Merriam-Webster's website, an apology is an admission of error or discourtesy accompanied by an expression of regret. Learning how one is sincerely regretful of how they hurt or offended the other repairs emotional feelings and relationships that create healthy and positive awareness. The apology you never received is the very apology you will now read as I sincerely regret that your feelings were never acknowledged and respected prior to this point.

Dear Beautiful Heart,

God says in his word that you are fearfully and wonderfully made in Psalms 139:14. You have a purpose, and the more you become a whole person, the more you will know and fulfill what that purpose is. Even better, the more you come near God, he will come near to you, eagerly awaiting for you to cast your cares to him in exchange for his strength, wisdom, peace, and so much more that will allow you to forgive!

I'm so sorry but also ecstatic that you are even reading this book. I say ecstatic because it shows that you are ready for closure, a pure heart, and in need to forgive others, yourself, or both. Other people may need to forgive you for things that you have done. I am sorry that you have been betrayed, lied to, dismissed, overlooked, or rejected. I'm sorry that the people closest to you took you for granted or never saw your worth. I'm tremendously sorry that no matter how hard you tried to work on those relationships and no matter what you did, you were always made to feel like it wasn't good enough or you were not enough. You didn't deserve any of the abuse you've had to endure, whether it was mental, verbal, or physical.

I am so sorry that you are struggling to love yourself or love others due to trust issues and pain. I pray that this book helps you to forgive so that you can be free to be all God has called you to be. I pray that, through reading each testimony, you were encouraged all the more knowing that you can genuinely love someone who once hurt you so badly and that it is possible to forgive and still keep the one who hurt you in your life—if it's the Lord's will. I pray that each testimony has renewed your courage knowing that it is possible to forgive and let go, to move on from a toxic environment, and to go where you're truly loved, valued, and appreciated.

Unforgiveness is a poison that doesn't kill the other person; it kills you if you don't deal with it. The enemy wanted for so long to silence my voice by attacking and smothering me with overwhelming hurt, deceiving me to feel like there was no way out. However, God showed me that forgiveness is the way out. It was the way out for me, and I can attest with confidence that it is the way out for you, too. I know your desire is to be set free because you chose to read this book with intent to no longer be bound by hurt or failing relationships.

As you are learning to truly forgive, it will bring you freedom and an ultimate reconciliation back to God. You cannot truly hear His voice when you carry all those burdens on an unclean heart. If none of your offenders ever apologize, please take my apology in place of the one you may never receive. I am so sorry for your pain and the trouble it has caused you. By your faith that has brought you to this point, I believe God will get you through this, which is why I couldn't be more happy and proud to acknowledge and confirm that you are now on your way toward the necessary path of complete healing, in Jesus' name. Amen.

Love Unconditionally,
Bridgette Alese Ferguson

Let's be honest—there are moments when forgiveness can be easy and other moments when it can be extremely hard. Bridgette has found that though forgiveness isn't always easy, it is very necessary, even if you never got an apology you should have received. When you choose to put God first by loving him with all your soul and obeying his commands, wanting to forgive others just as he has forgiven you for all your sins will become necessary for your salvation, necessary for your ability to hear his voice, and necessary for your heart to remain free and pure as you seek to please and be close to God. It's harder for Him to fill us with the right things if we are full of the wrong things—especially unforgiveness.

About the Author

As Bridgette's desire to be closer to God became stronger, so did her desire to be unlike the people in Isaiah 29:13 saying, "The Lord says: These people come near to me with their mouth and honor me with their lips, but their hearts are far from me. Their worship of me is based on merely human rules they have been taught." She knew it was time to pray to God for a new heart. She realized she could fake it to people but she couldn't fake it to God. She could even fake it to herself and choose to be in disbelief about changes that need to be made, but the word in Daniel 2:22 says, "He reveals deep and hidden things; he knows what lies in darkness, and light dwells with him." Through one of God's commands to forgive others, Bridgette not only found peace and joy but also found her confidence with clarity and revelation in her identity and purpose in Christ.

As instructed by God to write this book, Bridgette

believes renewed hope and healing will take place in your heart as you read each powerful testimony and receive each apology you never got. As you pray and allow God to search your heart and deal with those hidden things (unforgiveness, resentment, anger, fear, rejection, envy, hurt, jealousy, and more), may the Lord give you a new heart and put a new spirit in you, removing from you a heart of stone and giving you a heart of flesh, according to Ezekiel 36:26, so that you can truly worship, please, and serve God to the divine fullest.

Born at Duke Hospital in Durham, North Carolina prematurely, her mother only knowing about and being able to prepare for four months prior to her early arrival, Bridgette believes she was placed here on earth with a great purpose from God. He soon confirmed that by allowing her to break family generational curses, starting by completing college at Winston-Salem State University with a Bachelor's Degree in Mass Communications, Radio and Television Sequence to becoming a music-driven television producer/multi-media personality for Viacom Networks and her own worldwide online talk show, The Bridgette Alese Show. Now as a servant of God, wife, mom, and founder of Beautiful

Hearts, Bold Attitudes, Inc., she has a passion to help God's people by interceding, encouraging, mentoring, and allowing God to use her however he sees fit by the power of the Holy Ghost that is within her.

www.ingramcontent.com/pod-product-compliance
Lightning Source LLC
LaVergne TN
LVHW041635070426
835507LV00008B/628